Harriet Lane
First Lady of the White House

By Ginger Shelley and Sandie Munro

Harriet Lane

First Lady of the White House

Dedication

To Jim, Justin, Jordan, and Jaden and to Leo, Julian
and Cole.

Table Of Contents

Chapter One

A Visit From Nunc

On a bright summer day in the busy country hamlet of Mercersburg, Pennsylvania, the Lane family was preparing for the arrival of their uncle, James Buchanan. The whole family always looked forward to these visits from Uncle James. He always had so many interesting things to tell about, and he and Jane Lane, Harriet's mother, had such a good time when they were together.

Harriet was the youngest of the four children and her uncle's favorite. As usual, she was just a little impatient; waiting for his arrival was so hard! Everyone else in the family seemed to have something to keep them busy, Harriet thought as she wandered about with nothing to do. Father was just finishing his work in the store. He had a thriving business because their store was on the main road from East to West. Mother, even though she was not feeling very well, was preparing the meal they would have together. At the moment she was baking apple pies. Mary Elizabeth was old enough to help and was giving Mother a hand with the preparations. Ten-year-old Elliot and his older brother James had run out to meet Uncle James's coach.

Harriet wandered over to the window where she could get a better view of her uncle's arrival. "Your Uncle James is a very important lawyer in Lancaster and is now a United States Senator," she heard her mother telling Mary Elizabeth. "Everyone thinks very highly of him," her mother continued. Harriet could understand why. Uncle James was so tall and handsome and was always dressed so well when he came to visit.

On this visit Mother and Father were going to have a special talk with Uncle James. Harriet wasn't exactly sure what a guardian was, but she had heard her parents saying that Uncle James was going to be hers. If anything ever happened to her parents, he would make sure she and her sister and brothers were properly cared for and received a good education. Harriet and Mary Elizabeth were still little girls. There was much sickness in the family. Aunt Harriet had come to live with them before she died, and now her son, Harriet's cousin, James Buchanan Henry, lived with Uncle James.

Harriet gave another sigh of impatience. It was so hard to be still on this beautiful day! If only she could find something interesting to do without getting into trouble. Harriet looked around the pleasant, well-furnished room. She liked Mercersburg where she lived since she was born in 1830. There were always lots of visitors, and father's store was especially fascinating. Although she wasn't allowed in the store very often, occasionally father treated her to a short visit. She enjoyed listening to the traders who came to the store to talk with her father.

Suddenly Harriet heard her brothers' delighted squeals. Uncle James must have arrived! In a flash Harriet thought it would be fun to hide! She quickly slipped outside and into the nearby orchard. This was going to be exciting!

Uncle James came into the house just as Harriet disappeared outside. He greeted Harriet's mother warmly and asked about her father. "He'll be along shortly," Mrs. Lane replied. Next he gave Mary Elizabeth an affectionate hug. "And now where is our little scamp?" he asked, looking around. "Harriet- Har-ri-et!" called Mrs. Lane sternly. She was always having trouble with her younger daughter. Why did Harriet have to behave like this just when Uncle James was arriving?

They all began to look for Harriet. Brothers James and Elliot searched upstairs. "She must have gone outside," said Uncle James. "I'll look for her in the yard. Harriet, Har-ri-et, where are you?" called Uncle James. Suddenly he heard a clear little voice above him. "Why Uncle James, you're here already!" Uncle James looked around but could not see Harriet. "Now Harriet, where are you?" he said, just a little annoyed. This young tomboy was up to her usual tricks. He really must have a talk with her. "I'm right above you, Nunc," said Harriet, affectionately using her pet name for her favorite relative. Uncle James peered up into the apple tree and saw Harriet perched on one of the branches. She had gathered a bunch of apples in her apron. Uncle James helped her down but was unable to avoid tearing Harriet's Sunday dress. "What were you doing up in the apple tree?" asked Uncle James with a disapproving tone in his voice. "Just gathering more apples so we can bake another pie," said the lively Harriet. Well, thought Uncle James, at least Harriet was honest and forthright. Mrs. Lane often mentioned Harriet's mischief in her letters to him, but Uncle James could see that Harriet was not a bad girl, just a little too lively.

"Well, young lady, come inside and clean up while I soothe things over with your mother. She won't be happy about your dress, I'm sure. Come along now," Uncle James continued as Harriet grabbed his hand and gaily approached the house. It was so nice to have Uncle James around for awhile.

Uncle James explained where he had found Harriet and soothed things over about her behavior. Harriet, using her very best manners, served him a big piece of pie that her mother baked earlier. Then she picked up some simple sewing that Mary Elizabeth had been teaching her to do and sewed quietly as she listened to her mother and Uncle James talk.

Being a lawyer in a busy town like Lancaster and having to travel because of his work, Uncle James had many interesting stories to tell. Harriet did not want to miss a word of what he would say. He had a very good law practice in Lancaster, and his business caused him to visit many places such as Pittsburg, Philadelphia, and Washington, D.C. Harriet especially like to hear about the social events that took place in the towns. Some of his law cases were even interesting.

Jane Lane told her brother about life in Mercersburg. They had both been born in nearby Stony Batter and grew up in this south-central Pennsylvania farmland area. Although James had moved to Lancaster, he kept close contact with his family and friends in Mercersburg. He was the oldest one in the Buchanan family and felt a responsibility to see that all was well with them. His sister Jane was not well, and that was why he wanted to talk with her about the guardianship and education of her children in the event of her death. It was not a pleasant task for him, but it must be done.

The visit came to an end all too soon. Uncle James would go back to Lancaster where a new law case awaited him. After saying his good-byes to the family, he leaned down and whispered in Harriet's ear. "Now try to be a good little girl for your mother," he said. "She gets tired easily and needs all the help she can get. Try to behave yourself for Nunc." Smiling at her uncle, Harriet said, "I'll try my very best." She meant it because she was always anxious to please her Uncle James.

Chapter Two

Harriet Moves East

Not long after Uncle James's visit, Harriet's parents died. Now she and Mary Elizabeth were orphans. Their brothers were now old enough to take care of themselves fairly well, but she and Mary Elizabeth were not. As was the custom in those days, the Lane children were sent to a relative's house until final arrangements were made for their care. The children went to Charles Town, Virginia (which became West Virginia in 1863), to stay with a relative of their father's until Uncle James came and made arrangements for their care and upbringing, just as he had promised their parents many months ago.

Uncle James was now their guardian. The girls had many relatives and could choose with whom they wanted to live. Uncle James would still be responsible for them in matters pertaining to their schooling. Harriet already knew that she wanted to live with Uncle James.

It would be nice to live in his home near the busy square in Lancaster. There would be so much for a little girl to see and do!

Uncle James arrived, and it was finally decided that Harriet would join him shortly. He had to purchase some additional furniture and get his house ready for his niece's arrival. He even bought a pinao for Harriet. The piano cost $17.50.

As she was packing her bag for the long trip to Lancaster, Harriet felt just a bit frightened inside. She missed her parents and remembered the many good times the family had had together. Uncle James was not married. He would not be used to having children around and under foot. He did not know family life as she knew it. Perhaps he was only doing this because he felt it was his duty to take her. Maybe he would regret the promise he made to her parents that afternoon at the house in Mercersburg.

The journey to Lancaster was long and tiring. The road was bumpy, and the stage coach lurched back and forth as it wound around South Mountain. Harriet held tightly to her hat with one hand and gripped the seat with her other hand. As they rounded the mountain she noticed that there were many ruts in the dirt road. Even though they were traveling one of the main roads in the country, it was pitted with holes, and the passengers inside the coach swayed and bumped against each other.

The ride became smoother as the stagecoach went up King Street toward the square in Lancaster. Harriet's heart gave a little flutter. She peered out the window and saw the two-story brick courthouse right in the middle of the square. This was a much busier place than she had imagined! Lining both sides of the street were many taverns and shops of all kinds. On the tavern signs were pictures of Indian chiefs, national heroes, grapes, and many animals. Swans, lions, leopards, bears, and eagles brightened the signs with their colorful figures.

The stagecoach came to a stop in the square, and the driver jumped down to tie the horses. He opened the door for Harriet and held out his hand to help her down from the high coach.

Harriet looked shyly around, wondering where Miss Hetty, Uncle James's housekeeper, was. Just then a pleasant-looking woman reached out to Harriet. "My poor dear child, you must be tired after all that traveling. Don't worry, you are almost home," she said as she pointed to a house just off the center of the square. "I've just bought some fresh tea cakes at the market stand. Let's go home and have tea together."

The thought of nice hot tea and tea cakes made Harriet smile. She tucked her small hand into Miss Hetty's and together they walked the few steps to 42 East King Street.

Because Uncle James was so busy with his law practice and his work as a United States senator, he was not often at his home in Lancaster. He had to spend much of his time out of town on important business. Harriet and her cousin, Jimmy, were left in the care of

Miss Hetty. Uncle James, however, did have definite ideas about the schooling his nephews and nieces should receive. Although Uncle James was a kind guardian, he proved to be strict on the subject of education. He sent Harriet to a day school taught by Miss Young. Her days were filled with school, trips to the market, and Sunday visits with Miss Hetty to St. James Episcopal Church. After church, if the weather was nice, she and Miss Hetty would often wander through the courtyard. Sometimes Harriet saw that Miss Hetty placed flowers on one particular grave. "Whose gravestone is that, Miss Hetty?" asked Harriet. "Just a friend of your uncle," said Miss Hetty. Harriet peered closer and saw the name Ann Coleman written on the stone. Harriet recalled hearing her family whispering about Uncle James's tragic love affair with Ann Coleman.

Ann's father, a wealthy iron master, wanted only the best for his daughter. He thought James Buchanan would never amount to much. Mr. Coleman disapproved of their engagement and sent Ann to Philadelphia where she would not see James. A few days after her arrival in Philadelphia she died mysteriously. James was very heartbroken and remained a bachelor all his life.

Throughout these years Harriet was a headstrong girl whose mischievous ways and curiosity got her into all sorts of trouble. The local people often commented on Buchanan's newest arrival and how she would mimic visiting politicians. Too often for his liking Harriet received bad reports from her school. He had been threatening to send Harriet to the Misses Crawford's boarding school in Lancaster. Now he was going to do just that. He hoped the strict discipline of the school would make Harriet settle down. But Harriet was not at all happy at the boarding school and begged her uncle to allow her to leave. Although she made many friends there, she complained of the strict rules, early hours, dress restrictions … and brown sugar in the tea!

Uncle James finally relented and sent Harriet to a boarding school in Charles Town, Virginia. Her sister Mary Elizabeth also attended the Charles Town School, which was run by their cousin.

At Charles Town, Harriet grew from a mischievous girl into a delightful young lady. She found her school subjects interesting, especially music. Uncle James was pleased with her progress in piano and social graces.

During the summer months, one of the things that Harriet liked to do best was visit Bedford Springs. It was a popular vacation place, and the springs were said to be good for your health. Here Harriet had the opportunity to meet young men her own age. One of her favorites was Henry Elliot Johnston.

To complete her education, James sent Harriet to the highly regarded Georgetown Visitation Convent in Washington, D.C. By that time Uncle James was the secretary of state in the administration of President James Polk. On Sundays Harriet visited her uncle and learned of the political events and questions of the day. She found her studies of history, astronomy, and mythology especially interesting and continued her progress in music. The convent was a well-known finishing school where young girls were taught the proper manners of society. Harriet was well-liked by the nuns and students for her intellectual abilities as well as for her lively personality. She also learned, under the guidance of the nuns, to be generous. She still was not as well disciplined as her Uncle James would have wished, however. Once she was reprimanded by a nun for writing a letter during class time to the young man, Henry Johnston, she had met at Bedford Springs. In her letter she included some geranium leaves that they had picked there together. Despite her relapses in behavior, she graduated with high honors from the convent school, and her uncle was very pleased. For years after she left the school, Harriet continued to write to the nuns.

Chapter Three

A Royal Visit

Harriet was eighteen years old now and had finished her schooling. She returned to Lancaster to help her uncle entertain the many important people he had come to know. She knew that he was very proud of her. She had changed from a high-spirited, mischievous imp into a lively, refined, intelligent woman. She enjoyed having a good time, but now she knew how to behave and still have a lively spirit. She and Uncle James understood each other very well. They had written to each other while she was in school. She confided in him, and he gave her friendly advice. He was also quick to scold her when he felt it was necessary. Sometimes he criticized Harriet's letters to him. Once he wrote: "Stiffness in a letter is intolerable The principal fault I found was in your not making distinct periods."

One day, shortly after her return to Lancaster, James announced, "Harriet, I feel that we need a larger house in which to entertain. I have just purchased a lovely home about a mile and a half west of the city. There we will be able to have large parties and enjoy each other's company." Harriet was delighted! She looked forward to pleasant evenings with her uncle, perhaps talking politics, playing the piano and reading journals together.

At their estate, known as Wheatland because of the many fields of wheat that surrounded it, Harriet had her first opportunity to show off her skills in entertaining. She looked forward to the many foreign dignitaries and political leaders who visited them often. In 1852 while they were at Wheatland, Franklin Pierce was elected president of the United States. He urged Buchanan to become the minister to the Court of St. James, which means that Harriet's uncle was being asked to become the ambassador to Great Britain.

Harriet was delighted. Now she would have a chance to see what British society was like. "Oh, Uncle, I am so looking forward to going with you to London! I will enjoy sightseeing and am interested in seeing the latest fashions," she confided in him one afternoon while they were together in the parlor.

Harriet was a little surprised and hurt when her uncle matter-of-factly replied, "I will send for you when I am ready." Poor Harriet! Again she was her impatient self, wanting to go directly to London with him.

She wrote repeatedly when he had gone, begging him to allow her to join him. Finally in the spring of 1854 she received a letter giving permission for her to come to London. Harriet resolved that she would do everything to make her uncle proud of her. And proud of her he was. When she was presented to Queen Victoria, her gracefulness and correct curtsy made such an impression that the Queen commanded Harriet be given all the courtesy that the wife of an ambassador would ordinarily have. Harriet and her uncle were to be good friends of the Queen and her family for years after.

Uncle James was not one to allow his niece to dwell on all the attention she received. Upon Harriet's receiving many compliments, he once informed the people of England that there were many girls in America who could equal Harriet's appearance and grace. This was not altogether true, however, for Harriet was stunningly beautiful with lovely violet eyes and a mass of golden hair.

Harriet did not let this special attention affect her. She remained her happy, vibrant self. She had a lovely personality and ready wit. Always honest, she made a pleasant companion and had many offers of marriage.

The days were busy, indeed, entertaining and being entertained. She had always been interested in fashion, and the style-conscious English society encouraged her to select her clothes with great care. She wore stiff crinolines, low necklines, and lace collars, known as berthas, falling from the neckline of her dresses.

But the fashions of the times were not her only interests. She also readily adopted many of the values of British society. She began collecting works of art, an interest she continued the rest of her life. Oriental and African primitive art was popular in Britain at the time. She had a strong interest in American Indians and introduced to Britain the Indian art native to her own country and in this way made a valuable contribution to the world of art. In England she also learned the value of social reform by learning how to play a part in changing things that needed improvement. The Industrial Revolution was at its height in Britain, and the need to improve conditions for the workers had made a great impression on Harriet. With many of her British friends, Harriet became active in this movement.

Always she was enormously popular. Uncle James and the famous poet Alfred, Lord Tennyson were to receive the honorary degree of Doctor of Civil Law from Oxford University. Harriet accompanied her uncle to the grand festivities. When the students at Oxford saw Harriet, they greeted this fashionable woman with cheers and much whistling. She became the center of attention at an event which was supposed to be for her uncle and the English Poet!

These years in England flew by quickly, and soon it was time to return to the United States. The Americans were eager to have them return. They were proud of the ambassador and his lovely young niece.

Chapter Four

The White House Years

Shortly after their return to Wheatland, Harriet was thrown into a whirlwind of more politics. Her dear Nunc was elected to the presidency! "I can hardly wait to entertain at the White House," Harriet told her friends. "It will be such a pleasure returning all the invitations that I had received while in England. Nunc will surely allow me the freedom to plan some lively events."

There was much excitement at Wheatland and in the town of Lancaster as Inauguration Day neared. On a snowy, blustery day in March the church bells in the city rang to announce that Buchanan and his party would soon be ready to leave Wheatland for the Lancaster train depot. Many people lined the streets near the square for a glimpse of Buchanan's carriage. Excitedly Harriet entered the carriage along with her cousin James and Miss Hetty. Trying to look her best,

Harriet adjusted her hat and peered ahead to see the specially decorated train waiting for them. She saw the brightly colored uniforms of the Lancaster Fencibles, who were local military volunteers, waiting to lead them to the train bound for Baltimore. There, the presidential party would change trains to complete the trip to Washington. "I hope the weather in Washington is more pleasant for the inauguration than it is today," Harriet said to her cousin James. "Nunc has not been too well lately and should not be parading about in weather like this." As usual, Harriet felt great concern for her uncle and was trying to take care of him.

Just as she was seating herself on the train headed for the capital, Harriet commented, "I wonder where the Fencibles are. They do not seem to be on board, and we have had a few hours layover." As the train pulled hurriedly out of the Baltimore station, the breathless group of Fencibles appeared on the platform. It seems that they were going to miss the festivities after all. On their march between stations they had an unexpected encounter that caused them to miss the train! Later they boarded another train bound for Washington.

Harriet was up early on Inauguration Day. "Oh what a lovely day!" she exclaimed to Miss Hetty as they were getting ready that morning, for March 4, 1857, had dawned bright and clear. As she joined her uncle for the parade, Harriet noticed that the buildings of Washington were draped with red, white, and blue bunting. American flags were hung from the windows. Leading the grand procession was a float drawn by six white horses. Mounted on the float was a statue representing the Goddess of Liberty.

After Buchanan took the oath of office, everyone began to prepare for the events that were to take place that evening. Harriet eagerly prepared for the Inaugural Ball. She looked lovely in her with dress decorated with artificial flowers. Miss Hetty helped her with the necklace with its many strands of pearls. Harriet's violet eyes sparkled brightly that night.

She was a young and beautiful first lady of the White House. It had been a long time since so young and lively a woman had been hostess there. She accepted her duties with an eager heart and much charm. The American people were captured by her winsome ways and her elegant entertaining. The dinner parties she planned were accepted well. Because of the amount of entertaining Harriet and her uncle did, Buchanan had a conservatory put into the White House to raise flowers for the events.

Now Harriet could repay the many kindnesses she and her uncle had received in England. Upon hearing that the Prince of Wales was going to tour British North America (now Canada), she and James Buchanan urged him to visit with them in the White House. The Prince of Wales and Harriet had become very close friends during her stay in England. What fun it would be to entertain him! He always loved a good time, especially dancing. There was much to do to get ready for the arrival of this future King of England. No other royalty from England had ever visited the United

States. Harriet planned his five-day visit with great care. She wanted everything to go smoothy.However, when she consulted with uncle about her plans to entertain the Prince, she was in for a disappointment. "What is this mention about a grand ball in the White House, Harriet?" asked Buchanan after looking over Harriet's schedule. "You certainly must be aware that many of my supporters still do not approve of dancing. We must remember that the White House is not our personal home but the home of all Americans. It would not be a good idea to have dancing here when so many people are against it." Harriet was disappointed. After all, she was still young and had ideas of her own. Satisfying herself with a dinner party, Harriet set to work planning it with great care.

When the Prince arrived, he greeted his friends warmly. They sat down to an elegant, formal dinner, but to Harriet's dismay, things did not turn out has she had hoped. Part of the way through the courses, she whispered to her uncle, "Look at the Prince, Nunc. Why is he falling asleep!" Hurriedly Buchanan ordered his waiters to serve the remaining courses quickly. Usually Harriet's carefully planned affairs were lively. What could have gone wrong? "We must do something about this, Nunc," she continued, for the Prince's unseemly behavior was causing her great distress. Very reluctantly her uncle finally permitted Harriet to continue the evening's entertainment with some card playing, hoping to satisfy the young people.

After a bit of card playing, the guests settled down for the night. "Thank you so much, Uncle, for the lovely evening," said Harriet. "I know the Prince would have preferred dancing because he kept inquiring about it. However, as it turned out, the card playing proved to be fun for us all." She and her uncle returned to their rooms for the evening. Unfortunately for Buchanan, he was not to have the rest he well deserved. Upon arriving at his bedroom, he found that it was already occupied by one of the many guests. There were so many guests to be placed, that President Buchanan had to sleep on the sofa that night with his Newfoundland dog, Lara, nestled beside him.

The next day Harriet and the Prince toured some public buildings and went to a reception. Harriet, always ready for some fun, invited the Prince to a gymnasium, where he enjoyed himself by swinging on the rings and climbing rope ladders. He and Harriet ended the afternoon with a challenging game of nine pins, which Harriet won.

The highlight of the Prince's visit was a trip down the Potomac on the steam cutter, U.S.S. Harriet Lane. The group had lunch on the deck, and there was much music and dancing. They docked at Mount Vernon, and the guests had a magnificent view of the Potomac and nearby Washington, D.C. The Prince of Wales placed a wreath on the tomb of George Washington and gave a speech. This simple ceremony was the beginning of a new relationship between America and Great Britain. The pain of the Revolution and the War of 1812 were forgotten, and from that time on Americans could rely on Britain as a strong ally. Harriet could be proud of the part she played in restoring this friendly relationship between the two countries.

Chapter Five

Indians, Art, and So Much More

Although busy with her entertaining, Harriet had many other interests while living at the White House. In 1857 she supported a movement to create a national art gallery. She continued her own collection of art, and many of her parties and dinners included as guests people who were knowledgeable in the arts.

Another important concern that Harriet had was that of the American Indians, which she had promoted during her years in England. Now she was called "Great Mother of the Indians" because of the work she did to help improve their living conditions. The Indians appreciated this concern, and soon there were many Indian girls named Harriet!

Many other people honored Harriet at this time, too. The popular song, "Listen to the Mockingbird," written by Septimus Winner, was dedicated to her. The government steamer that was used to entertain the

Prince of Wales on his trip down the Potomac was named for her. The Prince sent Harriet a set of engravings of his parents as a gift upon his return to London.

People were very pleased with Harriet's popularity with royalty and foreign dignitaries. For the first time the White House was honored with a visit from a Japanese ambassador. His gift to Buchanan was a lovely, large oriental bowl.

There was little, if any, criticism of Harriet. Perhaps her greatest mistake, an innocent one, occurred on a visit to New York. The U.S.S. Harriet Lane was docked in New York harbor, and she was invited to tour the steamer named in her honor. She took the opportunity to invite a group of friends to go along with her. They held a delightful party on the boat, only to be sternly reminded by the press and her uncle that the boat was government property and not a place for private entertaining.

Although Harriet was making a very favorable impression on the American people, Buchanan was having a difficult time as president. There was friction between North and South over states' rights and the issue of slavery, and in the last months of Buchanan's presidency, southern states began to leave the Union. Harriet, as always, was a great source of comfort to her uncle. She was quick to defend her uncle's policies, feeling that he was trying to do the proper thing at all times.

Now that his term of office was nearly over, Harriet busied herself with the preparations necessary for their return to Wheatland. "I will look forward to the peace and quiet of our lovely country estate," she confided to Miss Hetty. "Uncle will be busy writing his memoirs, and I shall have time to visit my friends." And Harriet did just that.

Chapter Six

Family Life in Baltimore

While in Baltimore Harriet renewed her acquaintance with Henry Elliot Johnston. Many, many years ago, while still very young, Harriet had met Henry while vacationing at Bedford Springs. In fact, those same geranium leaves were still in her possession after all these years! In October of 1864 she and Henry announced their engagement. Uncle James readily approved. He was happy in Harriet's choice of a husband.

On a cold, snowy day in January, 1865, with Harriet's uncle, the Reverend Edward Buchanan, rector of Oxford Episcopal Church, conducting the service, Harriet and Henry were married. Warm fires glowed and flowers from a local greenhouse filled the rooms at Wheatland. After a lovely honeymoon in Cuba, the couple settled in an elegant house that Henry had prepared for Harriet in the city of Baltimore. He was a banker there, and she would be quite happy among his family and friends.

A son was born to Harriet and Henry in November, 1866, and they named him for James Buchanan, the former president. Buchanan was getting quite old by now and was not well. He had lived long enough to see his namesake but, shortly thereafter, died at Wheatland. Harriet was greatly saddened by his death and was glad to have a family of her own to comfort her. Another son was born a short time later, in 1869, and was named Henry Elliot. Those years of marriage and motherhood filled Harriet's days with much happiness and comfort. Her husband encouraged her to continue her hobby of art collecting and these interests kept Harriet busy. Their home in Baltimore became a center of artistic activity. Occasionally she found herself writing letters to editors and politicians of the day who continued to criticize her uncle for his role in the years preceding the Civil War. She strongly denied accusations that he had accepted and kept gifts that were presents to the government. She would not let the American people have their minds filled with accusations that simply weren't true.

Harriet and Henry thoroughly enjoyed the next ten years of parenthood. They were wealthy and able to give their boys many benefits not available to most children at that time. The family enjoyed many trips in America and abroad. Harriet especially enjoyed the summers they spent at Wheatland. Little James and Henry romped around the wide lawns there. They played hide-and-seek in the big stately house and in the evenings gathered around their parents and listened to Harriet's tales of childhood. On summer Sundays the family would all go to downtown Lancaster for the worship service at St. James Episcopal Church.

Then came a very sad time in Harriet's life. Her boys had never been very healthy, and she spent much time trying to improve their health. But despite all her efforts, little James Buchanan Johnston died at the age of twelve. As a memorial to their young son, the Johnstons had a stained glass window dedicated to him and placed in Lancaster's St. James Episcopal Church. The archangel Michael in the window has a face which very closely resembles that of little James.

A year later the Johnston family went to France hoping that the warmer climate there would improve the health of their son Henry. However, the climate was of no help, and Henry died in France. Harriet and her husband sadly made their way home. On the trip back to the United States they talked about their boys. "What can we do to help other young children when they are taken sick?" Harriet asked her husband. "We have adequate finances," said Henry. "Let's arrange for a memorial to our boys." Harriet agreed, and the two of them thought and thought about what they would like to do. Finally they decided that the most appropriate memorial they could establish would be a hospital for children. It would be called the Harriet Lane Home for Invalid Children and would be in Baltimore. It was the country's first children's hospital. Now other children could have the specialized treatment and hospital care that their boys could not have. The Harriet lane Home is now associated with the famous Johns Hopkins Hospital in Baltimore.

Shortly after they had established this memorial to their sons another tragedy struck Harriet. Her husband, Henry died. Harriet was grief-stricken. She decided to sell Wheatland and her home in Baltimore. Then she moved to Washington D.C.

Chapter Seven

Harriet's Later Years

While in Washington Harriet became interested in the building of the National Cathedral. She was a loyal Episcopalian and watched with great interest as plans developed for this huge Gothic cathedral, which was begun in 1893. The cathedral would need choir boys for their services. She began planning for a school in which young boys would be trained to become choristers. Today this school, St. Alban's, is one of the best college preparatory schools in the United States.

During Harriet's years of widowhood she continued her interest in art. She wanted her private collection of art to be kept for the people of America. She continued to support the idea of a national art gallery. At her death, the Smithsonian Institution accepted her collection and formed the National Gallery of Art.

As Harriet grew older, she would often think about her life. She thought about coming to Lancaster as an orphan to live with her Uncle James; of all fun and pranks she had played while living in Lancaster; and of the schooling that Uncle James had so carefully chosen for her. Uncle James's love for her and his position in life gave her more opportunities than most girls can ever dream about. She hoped she had used them wisely as Uncle James had wanted. She remembered her fun in England and her friendship with Queen Victoria. Little did she know that in future years the span of her lifetime would be known as the Victorian Age, after her friend, the Queen. She also remembered the height of her life during the White House years and the opportunities she had for entertaining. These years at the White House gave her the chance to be influential in helping her country, and she dearly loved America.

Harriet died on January 13, 1903, at Narragansett Pier, a resort in Rhode Island. She was seventy-three years old and had been in ill health for some time. She was buried next to her husband and sons in Greenmount Cemetery in Baltimore. Newspapers across the country carried the news of her death. People were saddened at the news, but they would always remember how lovely she was as a first lady for America's only bachelor president.

EPILOGUE

Harriet Lane was one of the most popular and probably one of the most successful first ladies of our country. She used her influence and position to champion her interests in humanitarian reform and the arts.

Jacqueline Kennedy, first lady of the White House during the presidency of her husband, John F. Kennedy, used some of the ideas that Harriet Lane had previously pursued. During both administrations there was renewed interest in the arts. Jacqueline Kennedy also used Harriet Lane's idea of entertaining foreign dignitaries at Mount Vernon.

The Buchanan home, Wheatland, has been restored to its mid-nineteenth-century appearance. It is maintained by LancasterHistory.org - Lancaster County's Historical Society & President James Buchanan's Wheatland. It is recognized as a National Registered Historic Landmark. Wheatland is open Monday through Saturday 10:00 A.M. To 3:00 P.M. from April through October . It is located at 1120 Marietta Avenue, Lancaster, Pennsylvania. Phone: (717) 392-8721.

Important Dates

May 9, 1830	Harriet Rebecca Lane was born in Mercersburg, Pennsylvania.
About 1840	Harriet came to live with James Buchanan at 42 East King Street, Lancaster, Pennsylvania.
1848	Harriet graduated with honors from Georgetown Visitation Convent.
Spring 1849	Harriet and her uncle moved to Wheatland.
Spring 1854	Harriet served as hostess for her uncle who was the ambassador to the Court of St. James, London.
March 1857	Harriet moved to the White House as first lady for James Buchanan.
1860	Prince of Wales, the first member of the English royal family to visit America, visited the White House.
January 11, 1866	Harriet married Henry Elliot Johnston at Wheatland.

November 21, 1866	James Buchanan Johnston was born.
June 1, 1868	James Buchanan died.
1869	Henry Elliot Johnston, Jr. was born.
March 25, 1881	James Buchanan Johnston died.
Easter 1882	Stained glass window in St. James' Episcopal Church, Lancaster, presented by the Johnstons and dedicated to the memory of James Buchanan Johnston.
1882	Henry Elliot Johnston, Jr., died.
1883	Harriet and Henry E. Johnston incorporated the Harriet Lane Home for Invalid Children.
1884	Henry Elliot Johnston died.
January 13, 1903	Harriet died at Narragansett Pier, Rhode Island, at age seventy-three and was buried in Greenmount Cemetery, Baltimore, Maryland.
1904	A fund in Harriet's will established the St. Alban's Choir School.
1905	The Smithsonian Institution established the National Gallery of Art from Harriet Lane's collection.

Photographs are courtesy of
LancasterHistory.org

Harriet Lane's Children

Wheatland